EXPLORING

EXPLORING

USING 2x2 MATRICES TO ANALYZE SITUATIONS

RUTH WILLIAMS

iUniverse, Inc.
New York   Lincoln   Shanghai

Exploring
Using 2x2 Matrices to Analyze Situations

Copyright © 2007 by Ruth Williams

iUniverse books may be ordered through booksellers or by contacting:

iUniverse
2021 Pine Lake Road, Suite 100
Lincoln, NE 68512
www.iuniverse.com
1-800-Authors (1-800-288-4677)

Because of the dynamic nature of the Internet, any Web addresses or links contained in this book may have changed since publication and may no longer be valid.

The views expressed in this work are solely those of the author and do not necessarily reflect the views of the publisher, and the publisher hereby disclaims any responsibility for them.

ISBN: 978-0-595-42420-7 (pbk)
ISBN: 978-0-595-86755-4 (ebk)

Printed in the United States of America

To Di

CONTENTS

ACKNOWLEDGMENTS

My thanks to many people who have made contributions to my work:

To Di Sercombe, to whom this book is dedicated: as part of her drive to learn, she required that I describe the current situation and the possible actions we could take clearly and concisely and explored the implications of those actions. Her perseverance and penetrating observations have caused me to capture thinking and explore further; in other words to establish causes and possible outcomes as a routine exercise.

To the many friends and colleagues who have been catalysts for my thinking and have offered constructive feedback over the years, the most persistent of whom are Carrie Battaglia, Robert Crawford, Jacqui Ferguson, Kim Hart, Steve Heidt, Kaye Jones, Gareth Jones, Linda Riely, Debbie Peedin, Amanda Roberts, Kathy Shears, Bill Thomas, Gareth Williams, and Jen Williams.

To the editorial staff at iUniverse who have offered such valuable guidance.

Thank you.

PREFACE

This book is the output from exploring problems or complex situations that are potential problems. My career has outwardly been varied but with a strong common thread of assessing root causes of failures—of machinery, processes, or organizations.

In a breakdown situation, there are usually a few common attributes:

- The undesirability of the situation is very clear.

- The cause of the problem is generally unclear.

- There are a great many people involved.

- Many of the people involved believe they know what's wrong (and it generally isn't them).

- No one can summarize the situation; there are many views involved.

The circumstances also mean that the people involved are often angry or upset and feel threatened. An independent assessor coming onto the scene can cause these feelings to escalate. It is essential to keep the analysis professional and fact-based.

When you are faced with a crisis, you need to be able to understand it, explain it, and analyze what has caused it to occur. You also need to be able to separate out the symptoms from the root cause, as you generally need to fix both. And, as I have explained, you often need to present yourself credibly to people who are very stressed and sensitive to criticism.

Few crises are caused by a simple failure—most are a complex interweaving of immediate causes based on deeper causes and often complicated by failed attempts to remedy early symptoms. It can be most valuable to break a difficult and complex situation into smaller parts, decide which of those are most pressing, and then analyze more deeply the components.

I experimented with how to describe complex intertwined situations clearly enough that they could be discussed, and found a 2x2 matrix analysis to be a valuable approach. A 2x2 matrix is a square divided into four equal quadrants, with a different situation described in each. Using 2x2 matrices has helped me to analyze and present thinking about a complex problem by dividing it up into smaller units.

By presenting the information simply, I have found that even the most difficult of dialogues can remain largely unemotional and focused on the topic.

CHAPTER 1

BUILDING A 2x2 MATRIX

How this book may help you

This book is all about exploring situations, and I have brought together a number of examples of exploring I have done. In some cases, this exploration technique helped resolve a particular circumstance. In others, the analysis was done after the event and was used as an educational tool. Perhaps it was used in a similar situation that occurred later.

A most important point, though, is that none of these answers is right. Each is just my analysis at that particular time. These answers are not offered here as the correct answers; they are offered as examples of how exploring a situation that is causing concern can be a valuable thing to do.

Observing and analyzing, especially in less stressful times, will improve your skills, and you will find yourself more able to use those skills in times of crisis. You will find it very helpful, both personally and professionally, to be able to use those skills when many others are less able to cope.

The methods I describe will help you to:
- Assimilate information quickly and clearly.
- Identify the key drivers of the situation.
- Propose consequences caused by any two of those drivers.
- Recommend actions that could address the symptoms or the cause.

And by doing this, you will be able to:
- Be objective and keep emotion at bay.
- Put some structure around challenging situations.
- Think about things from a different perspective.

1

Practice definitely helps, so don't get downhearted if the first few explorations you do are vague or of limited value. Keep going and make sure you record all your attempts. You will find yourself returning to one or two of them, and that will give you the indication of when you have made an original and useful start.

Why explore?

Have you ever experienced any of these situations?

- Something strikes you as odd.

- You get the feeling that "this has happened before."

- When an unexpected and serious situation arises, you wonder whether you could have seen it coming, and if you had, could you have prevented it or reduced its impact.

For instance, children have died after mistaking medicine for candy. In the 1960s in response to the deaths, childproof medicine bottle lids became common. Could these tragedies have been avoided if early signs of the ease with which children could open medicine bottles were made more visible and the consequences better explored? Maybe.

To continue with the example of childproofing medicine containers, there is evidence today of problems in that arena:

- Some children are able to open the child-resistant containers.

- Some adults are unable to open them, especially where probable child-strength is used as part of the barrier mechanism.

Therefore, recognizing early indicators of impending problems and creating a convincing argument to act *before* the consequences arise would create the ideal situation and is worth aiming for.

Another example to think about is when an early indicator of problems or possible failures is especially important—when the consequences of failure can be immediate and drastic. In the aircraft industry, near-misses are valuable sources of information. A "near-miss" occurs when two aircraft become closer than air traffic control staff intends. The term is widely used to mean "an accident that nearly happened." Near-miss situations help you to understand what could have transpired if circumstances had been different.

A situation in which disaster almost strikes provides the opportunity to learn without suffering the impact. If continual improvement is important to you, exploring varied situations and learning from them is imperative. This may mean exploring something that is odd or something that has a relevance that is not yet clear to you.

To expand further on exploring things that are odd or out of place, here is another example:

In the UK a few years ago, a television program called "Young Scientist of the Year" hosted a competition for teams of school children to demonstrate their scientific knowledge and abilities. The contest started with many schools competing to get to the next level, through quarter-finals and semi-finals, until a winner was declared.

On one occasion, the show featured a team that had noticed a small temperature change. The change had happened at the beginning of an experiment, but clearly was not the purpose of the demonstration. They had asked their teacher about the event they had noticed and were hustled along to complete the experiment that they were supposed to be doing.

They resisted their teacher's guidance and explored the small change. Their research revealed a repeatable phenomenon that had not been investigated or documented previously, not even by the scientists who had developed the experiment for use in schools.

The team won the overall prize that year in recognition of their curiosity and zeal to understand—important attributes of successful scientists.

This incident impressed on me the importance of recognizing small symptoms, paying attention to them, and being aware that they may be relevant—even part of the system—rather than just noise in the system.

So in summary, why explore?

- To avoid making the same mistake twice.

- To recognize mistakes before they happen or when they are just starting to happen.

To achieve insight into obscure elements of a situation, you need to be observant, question what is happening, understand why it is happening, and learn from early symptoms and near misses, however insignificant they may seem.

How to explore

There is value in having a specific method to explore situations, especially if you are going to share your explorations with other people. Keeping your method consistent helps both you and your colleagues to quickly assimilate information and to pinpoint the salient points of the exploration. The overall method I will be describing is as follows:

Describe	Observe the situation
	Decide on the key drivers
	Describe the situation you are exploring
Structure	Organize your information so that you can gather additional insights
	Expand your descriptions by further observation if necessary
Conclude	Explain the consequences of taking no action
	Propose actions to address any negative outcomes

I will generally polarize the situation, making it much more black and white than it probably is, but thereby locating the key drivers of the situation. This usually oversimplifies the situation, as difficult situations are rarely simple. However, the key point, from my perspective, is that by simplifying a situation and analyzing it in a simpler form, it is often possible to address parts of the problem, thereby reducing the impact of the situation. Each case needs to be reviewed to see whether reducing the impact is enough to relieve the problem, or whether further work to address the entire situation is necessary.

I present the information in a 2x2 matrix, placing the elements that cause the greatest impact to the situation along the top and the side, and placing the consequences in the four quadrants. Here is a complete matrix for a situation in which there were considerable tensions in an office. I will explain the situation in more detail in the pages following the matrix.

Aligned Objectives?

	No	*Yes*
Yes	**Trying to understand each other** You are likely to spend time trying to align your objectives as you each recognize the importance of the other's part in the wider picture. **Action** Understand why the objectives are not aligned (Is it a misunderstanding?) and address the situation as far as possible. Ensure that senior management is aware of the problem. If true misalignment is the case, the impact could be far-reaching.	**Working together well** You are likely to work well together and make good progress. Targets are likely to be met. **Action** Maintain.
No	**May not notice each other** Unless the objectives are contradictory and you are causing each other problems, you may find that you do not notice each other. **Action** Sort out the objective alignment first. Without that commonality, the possibility of establishing a shared view of relative importance seems unlikely.	**Competing for attention** If the prioritizations are seriously unsynchronized, emergency deliverables may be produced to meet commitments, causing impact to other work and possibly reducing quality. **Action** Explore why the views of importance differ. Is it a lack of visibility into each other's contributions? Is it a subsidiary effect from personal differences? Consider using organization-developing or team-building techniques to overcome the problem.

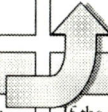

Same Priorities?

An explanation of how this 2x2 matrix was created

Describe

To start with, let's assume that you are confronted with a situation which is problematic: no one is achieving what they set out to do, and everyone is angry with everyone else, disengaged, or otherwise not working towards a successful conclusion. It isn't clear exactly what is going on, but there are squabbles over printer usage, mutterings about demanding colleagues, and generally an unpleasant atmosphere. We can assume that there must be an underlying cause because no one wants to be unhappy at work just for the heck of it.

The first step—observing—may be to note activities:

- *Who* is doing *What?*

- *When* and *Where* are they doing it?

- *Why* are they doing it and with what *Result?*

You don't need to record a complete list of activities. Just by watching, you will see that the main players will quickly become apparent. It will also become clearer what and where the problems are.

Watch, listen, and take notes. Look for things that fall into two categories: drivers and results. Maybe your list will look like this:

Drivers	Results
• Limited resources	• Refusal to cooperate
• Different objectives, perhaps contradictory	• Poorly done work—rework is likely
• Different priorities	• Resentment of time spent on other people's stuff
• Underlying jealousies	• Low personal job satisfaction

The drivers are the criteria that you might use to label the axes of your 2x2 matrix; the results are the items that you may put into the quadrants.

I might explore a 2x2 matrix of the things that I think would cause the most arguments. Looking at the list of drivers above, I am going to ignore "underlying jealousies." It almost certainly exacerbates the situation, but I don't believe I can do anything about it and must work around it instead. I am also going to ignore "limited resources." While there is no doubt that increasing resources (printers perhaps) would reduce tensions, I have decided that this is not the cause of the problem. The other two drivers are those that I will map:

- Along the top I can place "Aligned Objectives? Yes/No"
- On the side, I'll write "Same Priorities? Yes/No"

A 2x2 matrix emerges:

Aligned Objectives?

	No	**Yes**
Yes	**Trying to understand each other** You are likely to spend time trying to align your objectives as you each recognize the importance of the other's part in the wider picture. Consistently working in this quadrant can be expensive since you are spending time working on your team processes and not on the task at hand.	**Working together well** You are likely to work well together and make good progress. Targets are likely to be met.
No	**May not notice each other** Unless the objectives are contradictory and you are causing each other problems, you may find that you do not notice each other.	**Competing for attention** If the prioritizations are seriously unsynchronized, emergency deliverables may be produced to meet commitments, causing impact to other work and possibly reducing quality.

Same Priorities?

Structure

If there is a most desirable quadrant in a 2x2 matrix, and there isn't always, my personal preference is to place it in the top right position. In this example, I think that the ideal situation would be to have aligned objectives and the same priorities, so I place the two "Yes" answers so that the "Yes/Yes" quadrant is in the top right position.

Consider the possibility that if there is the best quadrant, is there also a worst one? Which quadrant is it?

Here are some notes about the various elements in the diagram:

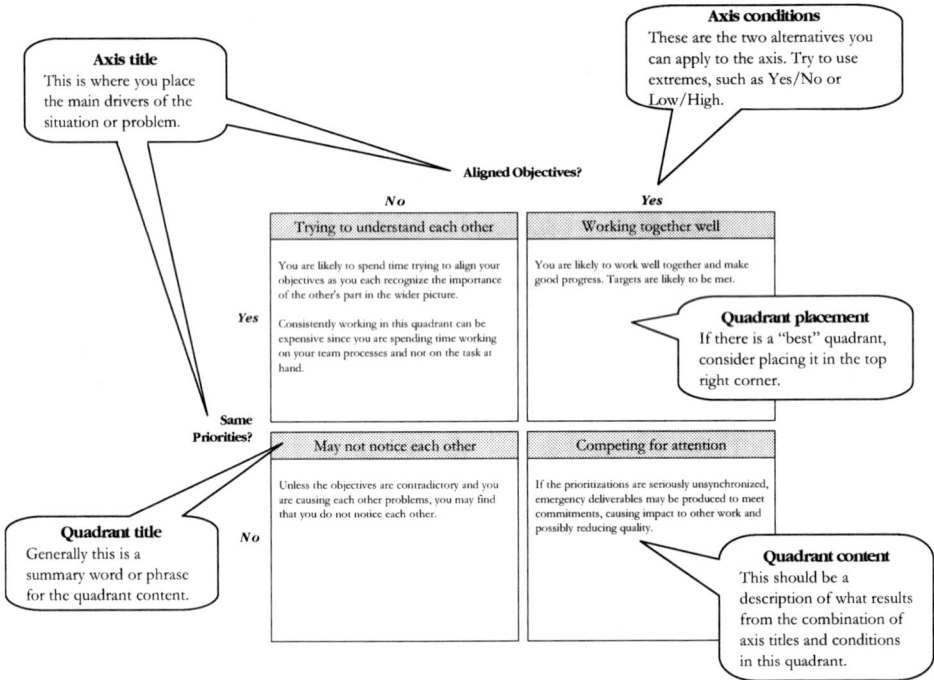

Axis conditions
These are the two alternatives you can apply to the axis. Try to use extremes, such as Yes/No or Low/High.

Axis title
This is where you place the main drivers of the situation or problem.

Aligned Objectives?

No   *Yes*

Trying to understand each other

You are likely to spend time trying to align your objectives as you each recognize the importance of the other's part in the wider picture.

Consistently working in this quadrant can be expensive since you are spending time working on your team processes and not on the task at hand.

Working together well

You are likely to work well together and make good progress. Targets are likely to be met.

Quadrant placement
If there is a "best" quadrant, consider placing it in the top right corner.

Yes

Same Priorities?

May not notice each other

Unless the objectives are contradictory and you are causing each other problems, you may find that you do not notice each other.

Competing for attention

If the prioritizations are seriously unsynchronized, emergency deliverables may be produced to meet commitments, causing impact to other work and possibly reducing quality.

No

Quadrant title
Generally this is a summary word or phrase for the quadrant content.

Quadrant content
This should be a description of what results from the combination of axis titles and conditions in this quadrant.

Conclude

So far, the matrix describes the behaviors that you have noticed, which has some value by increasing your awareness of the pressures people are under and the impact of the situation. To increase the value of the matrix, consider exploring further.

Ask, Then what? What needs to happen next? Who is going to do something different? What should we expect to happen, and what should we watch to ensure it does (or does not) happen?

Add these to your matrix under the heading "Action."

Aligned Objectives?

	No	*Yes*
Yes	**Trying to understand each other** You are likely to spend time trying to align your objectives as you each recognize the importance of the other's part in the wider picture. **Action** Understand why the objectives are not aligned (Is it a misunderstanding?) and address the situation as far as possible. Ensure that senior management is aware of the problem. If true misalignment is the case, the impact could be far-reaching.	**Working together well** You are likely to work well together and make good progress. Targets are likely to be met. **Action** Maintain.
No	**May not notice each other** Unless the objectives are contradictory and you are causing each other problems, you may find that you do not notice each other. **Action** Sort out the objective alignment first. Without that commonality, the possibility of establishing a shared view of relative importance seems unlikely.	**Competing for attention** If the prioritizations are seriously unsynchronized, emergency deliverables may be produced to meet commitments, causing impact to other work and possibly reducing quality. **Action** Explore why the views of importance differ. Is it a lack of visibility into each other's contributions? Is it a subsidiary effect from personal differences? Consider using organization-developing or team-building techniques to overcome the problem.

Same Priorities? (left axis label, Yes / No)

Assuming that there is a "best" quadrant positioned in the top right and you are in the bottom left quadrant—the one least like the top right quadrant—does it matter which way you go to get to the top right? If it does, which way do you recommend?

There are two factors to take into consideration:

1. Looking at the top left and bottom right quadrants, is one of these less desirable than the other?

2. Will it be easier to address one axis first?

In our example, the bottom right quadrant looks like an expensive place to be, so my initial thought was to make the priorities the same before aligning the objectives; in other words, move to the top left quadrant and then across to the top right quadrant. In practice, it would be difficult to have a conversation about priorities when objectives are misaligned, so despite the expense of the bottom right quadrant, the recommended approach is to align objectives first and sort the priorities out second, or move to the bottom right, then up to the top right.

You can see that the two considerations I mentioned above may be somewhat contradictory. You need to consider them both before making a recommendation.

In the 2x2 matrix below, I have marked the recommended direction with an arrow.

Aligned Objectives?

	No	*Yes*
Yes	**Trying to understand each other** You are likely to spend time trying to align your objectives as you each recognize the importance of the other's part in the wider picture. **Action** Understand why the objectives are not aligned (Is it a misunderstanding?) and address the situation as far as possible. Ensure that senior management is aware of the problem. If true misalignment is the case, the impact could be far-reaching.	**Working together well** You are likely to work well together and make good progress. Targets are likely to... **Action** Maintain
No	**May not notice each other** Unless the objectives are contradictory and you are causing each other problems, you may find that you do not notice each other. **Action** Sort out the objective alignment first. Without that commonality, the possibility of establishing a shared view of relative importance seems unlikely.	**Competing for attention** If the prioritizations are seriously unsynchronized, emergency deliverables may be produced to meet commitments, causing impact to other work and possibly reducing quality. **Action** Explore why the views of importance differ. Is it a lack of visibility into each other's contributions? Is it a subsidiary effect from personal differences? Consider using organization-developing or team-building techniques to overcome the problem.

Recommended Direction
When there is a better way to reach the ideal situation, use an arrow to make a recommendation on the matrix.

Action content
In addition to describing the results in a quadrant, add the action that should be taken to improve the situation .

Often, it won't make a difference which way you go around. And of course, you may be thinking "why go around at all? Why not jump straight from the bottom left to the top right?" If that is possible, then, of course, it would be a good thing to do. In my experience, one or the other of the axes will dominate the conversation, and you may prefer to make that dominance something you decide rather than something you experience by accident.

Polarizing your axes

Here is another example that demonstrates the benefits of polarizing the axes of your 2x2 matrix. One of the aims of polarizing your axes is to emphasize differences, thereby making alternative actions more visible.

To give you an example of this, I considered some features associated with exploring. In particular, I contemplated whether you should only ever attempt this exploration when presented with a crisis, or if there may be benefit in exploring at less stressful times. The polarization I used was:

1. Is the cause understood or not?
    Normally some of the cause is understood, but to polarize, force a yes or no answer.

2. Is the impact high or low?
    The impact may be somewhere in between or unknown; however, as part of the polarizing exercise, we will explore the situation as if the impact is extreme.

You can see in the resulting 2x2 matrix that, by forcing both criteria to an extreme situation, you tend to get four quadrants with distinctly different attributes. To recognize the likely attributes of less extreme situations, substitute less extreme terms, for example rather than "Yes" or "No" you can use "Some". The danger is that almost everything you examine will sit in the middle of the matrix and while this may be a truer reflection of reality, it is more difficult to identify a conclusion or an action.

Is the Cause of the Symptom Understood?

	No	*Yes*
High *Impacting our Business and our Ability to Work Together*	**Explore the cause urgently** It is important to explore the cause and understand what is going on immediately. **Action** If the impact to the business is high, action is needed. The better the situation is understood, the more likely the action will be successful and address the root of the problem.	**Explore possible actions to take** Once you understand the cause of the problem, you will be better able to resolve it. **Action** Assess possible options to ensure that the impacts of the proposed action are desirable, or at least not so undesirable that the current problems are preferable.
Low *Irritating, but Probably of Little Consequence*	**Explore the cause as time allows** If situation changes, the impact may become urgent. **Action** If you believe it is likely that the impact will increase, seeking to understand the cause of the problem before it becomes urgent would be worthwhile. It will allow you to gather other people's views without strong time pressure and to follow up on any other problems becoming visible.	**Opportunistic change** Knowing about an irritating symptom and understanding its cause may allow you to address it as part of another activity. **Action** Watch for opportunities to implement changes before they become urgent.

Impact of the Symptom

Going public with your explorations

I hope you can see the value of exploring systematically. I now want to encourage you to share your explorations and "go public." The value of the technique I have described is largely in the analysis and presentation of the exploration. You will often find that you are articulating things that everyone already knows. And there is the key word: articulating. Presenting a topic, possibly a controversial one, in a form that can be discussed and explored can add tremendous value for the people involved.

By sharing your observations, you will often encourage other people to comment and to challenge your analysis—improving the conclusions reached, and clarifying the actions needed. In some business or personal situations, sharing an exploration can be a viable and useful way to approach touchy subjects—the 2x2 matrix, rather than an individual, becomes the focus of any emotions.

It is important that you remain aware of your own emotions while exploring in a group. Remember that there are no wrong answers. There are alternative views, and new evidence may emerge. Additionally, try not to become too attached to your matrix—it may need to change to reflect new data or even be discarded.

The underlying tenet of this book is that exploring is useful; however, I have observed many situations where the exploring and thinking has been limited to elements that are directly and immediately relevant. In a crisis this is essential behavior, however when the crisis is over I suggest that expanding the exploring to related areas should be considered, as doing so may open up opportunities for change that might otherwise be overlooked.

Getting started

This book describes using 2x2 matrices to explore things. When creating these matrices for the first time, remember that it can take a few tries before the elements that really matter materialize. It would be a good idea to draw the initial attempts on a whiteboard or scrap paper.

You will probably find that consistency enhances your communications. As I mentioned when building the earlier example, if there is a most desirable quadrant in a 2x2 matrix, I prefer to place it in the top right position. Whatever your preference is, be consistent.

Often the relevance of a matrix will be short-lived. For example, recently a 2x2 matrix with about two hundred words on it was used as a working document for a meeting. It replaced two pages of detailed text and was a great deal clearer than the document it replaced. By using the matrix during the meeting, we could stay focused on the issue we had met to solve. Additionally, we could test the actions we agreed to take against the matrix and ensure that we had covered everything important. The matrix had limited value once the meeting was over.

When a matrix proves to be useful in a range of situations, it becomes part of the portfolio of matrices I use during my day-to-day work. Many of them are included here with some discussion of their usefulness in various contexts.

To make each matrix stand alone, and at the risk of being repetitive, each one is described thus:

- The circumstance that caused me to start the exploring process

- The key drivers

- The consequences of the situation, if left unaddressed

- The actions that could help the situation

The remaining chapters are used to group the matrices, though some of them would fit into more than one category. The categories are:

- Individual—related to behaviors of an individual or benefiting an individual

- Organizational—closely linked to an organization, but as organizations are made up of individuals, this is also a source of information for personal exploration

- Situational—associated with circumstances or with the overlap or collision of organizations.

My purpose in sharing these explorations is twofold:

1. The matrices may be useful in and of themselves. They may describe situations that you encounter and give you insight as to how those situations may be better managed.

2. Reading many variations of 2x2 matrices will enhance your understanding of their potential and increase your ability to create useful ones based on your own experience.

CHAPTER 2

INDIVIDUAL

Delegation styles

Context: I observed a colleague giving small tasks to a subordinate who was almost fainting with frustration and very unhappy. Both people were having problems with the other.

The boss preferred to keep control of situations and, unless she was very confident in her subordinate's ability, tended to delegate at a task level. The person she was delegating to preferred to work with a bigger picture, to see the entire context of what he was being asked to do and then decide how to do it. He preferred to be delegated goals.

Key Drivers:

1. Delegation preference of the delegator—to delegate tasks or goals

2. Delegation preference of delegatee—to receive work as tasks or goals

   Task level delegation: a short-term, limited-risk piece of work, with the method of achieving the outcome clearly described.

   Goal level delegation: work with a longer term horizon where the methods used to achieve the desired end points are not proscribed and where the responsibility of the delegatee is to manage the risk.

Consequence: The subordinate persisted in asking for the bigger picture, which the boss resisted. In fact, she started to break things into yet smaller pieces before delegating. They both felt threatened and unhappy. The situation was deteriorating.

Action: Luckily, circumstances arose that helped to address the situation and give insight into how such a situation might be remedied.

I was asked to draw up a plan for a large project. This plan eventually became a source of tasks to be assigned to the poor man. Of course, he was finding it very difficult to simply deliver results from a task list with little context.

I was able to pop into my colleague's office and ask if she had the plan I had created and if she would give it to me. When I had it, I took it to her subordinate and set it on his desk. He then saw the context and the desired end state and could decide on the best way to achieve it. Inevitably, he was able to improve on the tasks that were initially included in the plan.

Further commentary: My colleagues were working in the top left quadrant of this matrix, and the value of intervention in the situation became very clear. When the situation had calmed down, we were able to discuss it openly, using a matrix as a foundation.

Preference of Delegator to Assign ...

	Tasks	*Goals*
Goals	**Frustration** The delegatee is likely to be unhappy and will feel confined, restricted, and underused (or inappropriately used). His reaction is likely to be rebellion. If the organization is lucky, it will be within the organization and addressable. The risk that the employee will quit is high, especially if it persists. The delegator is likely to feel threatened. **Action** Consider intervention. Ask a colleague for guidance. A catalyst is often necessary in this situation.	**Growth** Individuals in this situation are likely to be the highest performers, as several minds are engaged in delivering the required end result. This situation is most likely to enhance individual skills, provides the goals are sufficiently stretching. **Action** Maintain
Tasks	**Contentment** Within the status quo, the arrangement will work well. There is unlikely to be much opportunity for growth, as the areas explored will largely be those the manager considers important. In many departments, this situation will be efficient. In others, it will risk limiting the individual's potential. **Action** Use performance reviews to discuss growth potential and avoid stagnancy.	**Confusion** The delegatee is liable to be confused and worried. If the situation persists, he may become stressed, though he may also grow to develop a preference to receive goals. Performance may be poor, especially if the delegator does not recognize the problem in a timely manner. **Action** Recognition of the challenge is key. The delegator should ensure that a mentor or coach is available to supply on-the-job advice.

Preference of Delegatee to receive ...

Who can mentor me?

Context: A previous employee called me in despair, bewailing that her new boss was driving her crazy. She couldn't explore anything with him. As soon as she opened a subject, the conversation turned to something more immediate.

Key Drivers:

1.   The type of challenge someone is seeking help with: a specific problem or a more hypothetical situation, perhaps development of a new concept.

2.   The preference of the mentor to explore the problem conceptually or to offer immediate help.

Consequence: In this situation, I propose that there is only one difficult combination—the one which initiated this matrix's creation—where a mentor has a more focused view than the person he is mentoring. In this case, the frustration can be extreme.

Action: If you are in the top left quadrant, then a change in mentor is probably needed. Elsewhere, no immediate action is needed, though some cautions are mentioned in the matrix.

Over the years, I have observed people's mentoring preferences many times, and the preferences appear to be very strong and difficult to change. If you are considering taking no action and simply hoping that things will improve, this persistence of preference is something you should consider.

Further commentary: Your boss is always one of your mentors. You may also have mentoring relationships with other people. If your preferences are mismatched with your boss's, especially if you are in the top left quadrant, you may be able to manage the situation by seeking an additional mentor. You may also need to face up to the possibility of changing your boss and even your employer if you are to achieve your full potential.

Mentoring Need

	Challenge or Problem is Unclear	Challenge or Problem is Clear
Narrow Focus *Prefers to Help with a Specific Problem*	**Bad match** There is probably very little value in discussing this problem. **Action** Get more focus on your requirement and identify specific items you need help with. Alternatively, seek another mentor to help you with your broader challenge.	**Good match** You'll get answers, but you may only get answers to the very specific question you have asked. **Action** No action is needed in the short term, however this is potentially a stagnant arrangement. You may want to seek an alternative mentor who would challenge you to a greater degree.

Mentor Preference

	Challenge or Problem is Unclear	Challenge or Problem is Clear
Broad Focus *Prefers to Help with a Concept*	**Good match** This mentor can work through your concerns with you and help you to find clarity on your issue. **Action** No immediate action is needed. The danger of a good match in this quadrant is that you will spend a great deal of time theorizing and not much time taking action.	**OK match** A mentor who works best with broad challenges may well seek to open your issue beyond your specifics, which may be helpful, but this may also mean that you don't get adequate help with your specific problem. **Action** If the specifics are important, you may need to seek another mentor to help you address your immediate challenge.

Personal versus organizational effectiveness

Context: I get annoyed when I find myself spending excess time doing something because of the way a task has been presented to me, when a bit more thought and action on the sender's part would have saved me a lot of time.

Electronic documents are a good example. The United States and Canada use letter-sized paper. The rest of the world uses A4 paper. If you try to print a document of the wrong size, it can cause printers to stop, though there are a large number of printers now that just carry on regardless. Think of the cost for all the recipients to have to resize the document or deal with stopped printers.

Key Drivers:

1. Organizational efficiency or effectiveness.
2. Personal efficiency or effectiveness.

Consequence: Individuals will naturally tend to do their best within their immediate area of control, seeking to maximize their personal efficiency. If this is done without thinking about the wider organization, lower efficiency in the wider organization may result.

Action: Review both personal and organizational efficiencies, and ensure that the balance is considered. To pursue the electronic documents example, if the sender had included two documents—one of each size—it would have been marginally less efficient for them, and more efficient for many of the people who received it.

Further commentary: This situation is exacerbated by the intuitive conclusion that if every individual maximized their personal efficiency, the organization as a whole would be at optimal efficiency. The purpose of the matrix is to challenge this assumption and to encourage individuals to consider the organizational impact when they make daily decisions.

While the top right quadrant represents the best situation, practice caution in aiming for it. Don't overshoot and end up in the top left quadrant.

**Organizational Efficiency
or Effectiveness**

	Low	*High*

	Low	High
High	**Lost opportunity** This may well feel fine to an individual, but this is a pointless place to be. An individual may be efficient while an organization is failing and is on the road to disaster. **Action** Review how you do your work, putting organizational effectiveness first and personal effectiveness second.	**Ideal** To have high personal effectiveness and to be supporting the efficiency and effectiveness of the organization makes this the most desirable of the four quadrants **Action** Continue to improve the situation, putting organizational effectiveness first and personal effectiveness second.
Low	**Avoid** This state of affairs is not good for anyone. The situation may be hard to recognize, though it could be improved by establishing clear targets and a performance measurement system. **Action** Try anything, you probably can't make the situation worse.	**May feel wrong** While this situation may feel wrong, it may be the right place to be. For example, an individual doing something more than once, which is personally inefficient, may make the wider organization more effective. **Action** Verify that improving personal effectiveness is the right thing to do. Assess the impacts of improving personal efficiency or effectiveness— are they all positive?

**Personal
Efficiency or
Effectiveness**

Caution

"Boss says" versus personal accountability

Context: I was being driven mad by a particular person saying "boss says" constantly to justify her action or her decision or even her lack of action. Anyone using "boss says" to defend an action is effectively invoking their boss's power in their own defense. Perhaps they do not feel that the power they personally wield is strong enough for the audience.

Key Drivers:
1. Complexity of the challenge an individual has been tasked with.
2. Personal ownership of actions or opinions related to that challenge.

Consequence: This was a combination of a highly complex challenge and a manager failing to take personal ownership of her actions, leading to a lack of credibility for both her and her boss. The change she was trying to implement, which included policy changes, with the subsequent behavior and task-related changes necessary to effect the new policies was failing. Her boss was also part of the problem: he was accepting her behavior—though the full implications of it may not have been visible to him.

Action: In any such circumstance, the appointment of the person saying "boss says" needs to be reviewed. Additionally, the boss also needs to review his delegation methods and ensure that he is providing a good balance of support and delegated authority.

Further commentary: An initially unacceptable appointment can often be made successful with strong mentoring, especially if there is confidence that the person possesses an underlying ability and the experience valuable for growth. Recognize that the behavior and actions of the boss are key elements for the success of delegated work.

**Complexity of Activity
or Challenge**

	Low	High
	Appropriate	**High trust**
Justifying your Action or Position Personally	Colleagues will probably notice nothing in this situation. **Action** None needed.	Colleagues will hear that the employee is fully empowered. The employee will be demonstrating that she believes in the value of what she is doing and that she is supported by her boss. **Action** Maintain.

Accountability

	Confused	**Danger**
Justifying your Action or Position by Saying "Boss Says"	Colleagues may be confused as to why the boss's opinion is particularly relevant in a trivial situation. They may conclude that the employee is not trusted by her boss. **Action** The employee should stop referring her boss and take ownership of her actions and opinions. The employee and her boss should explore trust.	Colleagues will hear that the employee is not fully empowered. The employee will be demonstrating that she does not believe in the task she is undertaking and that she is not supported by her boss. **Action** The employee should use 'boss says' sparingly. The employee and her boss should explore trust and competencies. The boss should consider the correctness of the appointment.

Decision type and power of decision-maker

Context: This matrix is based, in part, on Victor Vroom's work on types of decisions. Three of the categories of decision that he discusses are considered.

1. Autocratic—the decision-maker makes the decision. This is effective if they have the power to implement it.

2. Consultative—the decision-maker seeks opinions then makes the decision. This also requires high power.

3. Group—the group makes the decision. This is a necessary course to take in a position of low power (Vroom 1973).

Key Drivers:

1. The type of decision being made (autocratic or collaborative)

2. The power of the decision-maker

Consequence: If there is a mismatch—for example, a low-power person is trying to make an autocratic decision (bottom left quadrant in the matrix)—the decision may be rejected even if it is a good one.

Action: Review the key drivers, particularly for a complex or high-risk decision, and ensure that a good balance is arrived at.

Further commentary: It can be valuable to indicate which type of decision process is being used (*we* are making the decision or *I* am making this decision) to avoid confusion. A consultative decision is a mixture of collaborative and autocratic and will feel collaborative if your opinion is reflected in the decision and autocratic if it is not.

Dissatisfaction can occur when a group of people have been involved in a collaborative decision process, but have mistaken a consultative decision for a group decision. The decision-maker, in making a consultative decision, has listened to the opinions of the group and then made the decision, but the decision may not reflect all or any of the opinions aired.

Avoid the bottom left quadrant if you possibly can.

Type of Decision

	Autocratic	*Collaborative*

	Just do it	**Consultative**
High	This form of decision making is fast and effective. An individual continually working in this space may find it difficult to have cooperation in any other situation. **Action** If an autocratic decision is possible, economically it is desirable.	A consultative decision-making style can help to introduce change and ensure various opinions are heard. This form of decision making can be unnecessarily slow and can cause confusion when someone with high-power is asking for opinions, especially for apparently trivial decisions. This behavior can erode the person's power. **Action** Ensure you differentiate between a consultative decision, where you seek views before making a decision, and a group decision.

Power of Decision Maker
Context Specific

	Ineffective	**Group**
Low	Decisions made in this quadrant cause delay and add noise to the system. If the decision is sound, it may still be rejected when a more suitable decision-making process is used. A person who makes a decision in this quadrant (perhaps in error or not recognizing the context) can undermine their credibility. **Action** Avoid this quadrant. To do this, you will need to understand your power relative to the circumstance you are working in.	Group decision making is generally effective, and gains commitment from those involved. It can be a slow process however, particularly if key players' availability is limited. Collaboration with inexperienced players can result in a suboptimal compromise. **Action** Agreeing to the decision criteria before you start the process can help to ensure a high-quality decision is reached.

CHAPTER 3

ORGANIZATIONAL

Assumed competency: boss and employee

Context: I am periodically asked to assess troubled situations and recommend actions to improve them. On one occasion, I was horrified at what I found: demoralization, anger, even despair. During the assessment, I interviewed many people and repeatedly found that the conversation deteriorated into a wall of silence, which was only punctuated with statements such as "that won't work" or "we won't be able to do that" in response to minor and easy-to-implement suggestions.

The situation was driven by the following circumstances:

- A key leader assumed that all of his subordinates, but for his favorite few, were incompetent, regardless of their actual competence

- Inadequate mentoring and support for people in their day-to-day job—no one was helping them to succeed and grow.

Key Drivers:

1. Assumed competence

2. Actual competence

Consequence: A failure spiral was in place. As a result of his assumption of the incompetence of his subordinates, the leader engaged in very specific behaviors, such as closed questioning, making demands, and issuing mandates. Coupled with the lack of mentoring and the fact that any risks that turned out badly immediately became fuel for the assumption of incompetence, the situation worsened. As time went on, people took fewer and fewer risks, and performance levels dropped lower and lower, reinforcing the correctness of the "incompetent" diagnosis.

Action: The complexity of the situation requires that two actions be taken if it becomes as serious as it had in this case. Firstly, the leader has to break his behavior and assume competence rather than incompetence. Secondly, an external mentor should be brought in to help the employees regain confidence.

"How can I assume competence?" asked the leader.

"I don't care what is in your heart or your head," I replied "but you can and must control your behavior." Behaviors that indicate assumed competence include asking open questions, making suggestions, and listening

Further commentary: Many employees were in the top left quadrant of the matrix, and some were sliding to the bottom left as the continual drain on their self-esteem led them to doubt their abilities and their judgment. The situation was driving a result that reinforced the assumption that was driving the behaviors.

While working on the recovery plan for this situation, I became convinced that failure spirals need to be broken in two places, not just one, if the spiral is to be reversed. If the person assuming incompetence changes their behavior and demonstrates an assumption of competence towards the employees, the speed of change will be slow, and maintaining this façade will prove very challenging. Far better to also address the other driver of the situation and ensure strong mentorship and support is in place. The importance of two simultaneous actions is very clear.

Competence Boss is Assuming
of Employee

	Low	High
	Anger	**Creativity**
High	The boss is likely to ask closed questions, deliver mandates, and make demands. The employee may well react with anger, avoidance, or resentment. He may ignore the boss and avoid explaining when there are misunderstandings. The results will be wasted effort and limited change to behaviors that often doesn't stick. **Action** The boss must change his behavior. The employee could seek a mentor.	The boss may ask open questions, make suggestions, and listen to his employees. The employee is likely to react with similar behavior. This combination makes high creativity possible. **Action** Maintain.
	Safety	**Danger**
Low	The boss is likely to ask closed questions, deliver mandates, and make demands. The employee may welcome this and comply with the boss's rulings. This will result in improvements in the current paradigm, introducing efficiencies. **Action** The boss should offer support to improve performance.	The boss may ask open questions, make suggestions, and listen to his employees. The employee is likely to be unsettled and seek closure and answers. The result will be limited progress and lost opportunities for efficiency. Problems may go unnoticed. **Action** The boss should offer support to improve performance. The employee could seek peer support with day-to-day tasks.

Actual Competence of Employee

An exercise to demonstrate the power of assumptions

This is an exercise based on the experience explored in the previous matrix, which I use with groups of leaders. While everyone is seated at tables in the same room, I explain to the whole room the situation as follows:

- Each person's PC is broken.

- Each has called for help.

- A technician has come to the office but can't fix the PC.

I then split the room in half and say to those on the left side of the room, "You will assume that this technician is incompetent," and to those on the right side, "You will assume that this technician is competent." After ensuring that everyone understands that all the PCs are still broken, I ask them to capture the questions they would pose to the technician.

The people seated on the left side—who are assuming the technician is incompetent—typically produce a long list of questions that are:

- Closed questions (can only be answered with yes or no)

- Accusatory

- Demanding

- Personally attacking the technician (usually towards the end of their list).

The people on the right side of the room typically produce a shorter list of exploratory questions, which share the issue—"what should *we* do?"—even questioning themselves, "have *I* done something that caused this problem?"

The only difference between the two groups lies in the attitudes and assumptions of their members.

Linking back to the matrix

The exercise demonstrates how assumptions influence behavior—how if you are assuming incompetence, you behave in a specific way. In the example described in the matrix, the manager allowed his assumptions of incompetence to affect his management of this situation and was thereby contributing to the poor performance of the team.

Having a vote versus having an opinion

Context: In business, "one person, one vote" is rarely true, and it shouldn't be. Some people have no vote, and some people have a vote that is taken much more seriously than others'. This ensures that the people with the experience and skill are those that most heavily influence the decisions and lead to a successful outcome.

If a mixture of voters and nonvoters attend a meeting, it can be helpful to ensure that this difference is understood by all the people involved. If you have been in a meeting which has been plagued with a continual refocusing by stating "let's take this off-line," then you may be seeing a side effect of this. In those circumstances, the "off-line" meetings will often be made up of the voters only: they are needing to isolate the topic to the key players in order to make progress.

Key Drivers:

1. The type of meeting: is it a discussion meeting, or have the players met to make a decision?

2. The players: are they voters or nonvoters?

Consequence: Where there is lack of clarity about the role each player has, there can be unnecessary noise, discussion, and confusion. Add to this the rejection someone feels when his vote is being ignored (when he doesn't, in fact, have a vote). Far too much energy gets spent on the meeting process at the expense of the meeting content.

Action: Make the ground rules clear from the beginning. Ensure that the people with a vote know it and either attend the decision-making meeting or adequately delegate their vote. Ensure that the people without a vote are aware that they are invited for their expert opinion and in support of the voting players.

Further commentary: This is a complex situation, and it is difficult to explain to someone that she has no vote without wounding her feelings. To do this openly, however, before or at the beginning of a meeting is both effective and courteous.

What about the person with the veto vote—the person who can overturn a decision? Will they retain that right even if they are not at the meeting? If they will, then those at the meeting cannot make a decision; they can only make a recommendation. If you, as the chair, believe that the meeting should be a decision-making one, the veto holder has to be there or agree to forfeit his or her veto vote. Talk about it with them explicitly in advance.

Type (or Phase) of Meeting

	Discussion	*Decision-making*

		Discussion	Decision-making
Type of Responsibility	*Voter*	**Risk of limited participation** If the meeting chair doesn't clearly state that all are equal in the meeting, there's a danger that the discussion will be limited and people with a voting position will not be challenged. **Action** Voting players should seek to encourage full participation and might achieve this by refraining from stating their views early in the meeting.	**Key players present** For a decision-making meeting to be successful, the necessary voters must be present. It follows that delegation of the role in a meeting must include delegation of the vote. Sending someone to the meeting to "report back" but without the power to vote is a waste of everyone's time. **Action** The meeting chair should be very clear about which voters are necessary to carry a decision and should ensure that they are present or have adequately delegated their roles. Otherwise, the chair should cancel the meeting.
	Non-Voter *(Opinion Holder)*	**Active participation** A discussion meeting is ideally a forum where all opinions are aired and heard. People who have been invited to participate as nonvoting experts should recognize the value their views have and be willing to share them. It is not an insult to have no vote; voting is an attribute associated with a function. **Action** Nonvoting members of a meeting should be prepared to offer their views.	**Noise** Having nonvoters as part of the decision-making process, as opposed to the information-gathering process, can add unnecessary noise to the system. A nonvoter that does not recognize himself as such may be bemused if his point of view is not carried when the decision is made. **Action** In a meeting of mixed voters and nonvoters, it is imperative that the chair of the meeting clarifies who has a vote and who does not.

Trust as evidence of organizational health

Context: This analysis arose from observing large numbers of "initiatives" being launched within an organization and wondering:

- Why are the initiatives launched?
- How do the initiatives get the energy to persist?
- Who pays for the initiatives?

It became apparent that many people in the organization had a very clear idea of their role and the output they had to deliver, but there was a limited amount of shared direction. No one really understood what other people were tasked with, and had no clear vision into the relationships between their roles

Initiatives were started up often because a specific output was necessary for an individual's success. They had neither the confidence that it was someone else's role to achieve this output nor the trust that it would be a high priority to someone else.

Key Drivers:

1. Clarity of your own role's purpose and vision
2. Objectives shared with other parts of the organization

Consequence: The worst combination is when *you* know what you want to achieve but have no shared targets with anyone else. This invites anarchy. This describes the circumstances in the bottom right quadrant and was where the organization in the context described above was largely situated.

Action: In this matrix, the order in which you fix the problem is very important. If you think that you may be in the bottom left quadrant, improve the shared targets before making individual roles clear. You don't want to slide into anarchy.

Further commentary: Goal-setting is a vital part of running a business. Providing people with personal goals is essential to ensure high performance, however this example stresses the value of setting them in the context of organizational targets, and how far-reaching the consequences can be if this structure is not in place.

Clarity of Your Own Role

	Not Clear	*Clear*
Yes	**Ambiguity** There is low trust in the organization, with overlapping responsibilities due to the lack of role clarity. Insularity prevents the sharing of best practices. Progress tends to be slow as ambiguity makes decisions difficult. Personal success is difficult to assess. Reworking occurs often as decisions are revisited because of ambiguity. **Action** Improve the clarity of each other's roles. Consider using organization-developing or team-building techniques to overcome the problem.	**Advancement** There is high trust in the organization with minimal overlaps of responsibilities and clear relationships. It is possible to apply best practice to all operations as there will be a willingness to accept suggestions from other parts of the organization. Progress can be swift as very little time is needed to ensure clarity. **Action** Maintain.
No	**Accidental** Is trust relevant in this organization? Is the organization relevant? Neither can be discussed when there are no common aspects to rally around. Progress will tends to be very slow as there is neither personal clarity nor organizational energy. The lack of structure can generate creative ideas, especially as normal boundaries may not be strong. Only fragmented best practice is likely to function. **Action** Establish some shared organizational goals and targets: why are you an organization?	**Anarchy** There will be very low trust in the organization as everyone will appear to be looking after himself first and only. There will be implicit overlaps in the organization as the lack of clarity of organizational goals will affect the interpretation of personal goals. Progress can be very fast as the players know exactly what they want to achieve and have no common commitment with their colleagues. Progress will generally be unilateral. **Action** Establish some shared organizational goals and targets: why are you an organization?

Shared Objectives and Vision (row labels: **Yes**, **No**)

Satisfaction versus dissatisfaction for the employee

Context: The matrix that follows puts Frederick Herzberg's theories into a 2x2 matrix for ease of discussion (Herzberg 1959).

Herzberg proposed that satisfaction and dissatisfaction are not opposite items, but they reflect different ranges of human needs. He established two groups of things that affected employees' satisfaction or dissatisfaction:

Herzberg's Motivators: elements that increase satisfaction include:

- achievements
- recognition
- attraction of the work itself
- responsibility
- advancement

If these exist in adequate quantity and quality, your satisfaction (or motivation) increases. If these elements do not exist in adequate quantity or quality, you do not become satisfied or motivated—Herzberg's theory states that you would not become dissatisfied, just not satisfied.

Herzberg's hygiene factors: elements that cause dissatisfaction include:

- company policy and administration
- supervision
- salary
- interpersonal relations
- working relationships

If these do not exist in adequate quantity or quality, you become dissatisfied. If these exist in adequate quantity and quality, your dissatisfaction decreases. Herzberg's theory states that you do not become satisfied, you just become not-dissatisfied.

Key Drivers:

1. Dissatisfaction (related to hygiene factors)
2. Satisfaction (related to the motivators)

Consequence: By displaying Herzberg's theories in this way, you can see a paradox arise in which someone can be both satisfied and dissatisfied simultaneously. While this seems odd initially, let me give you an example. A friend visited me, and was very stressed. "I love my job!" she cried, "But I am so fed up with almost everything at work that I think I may leave." When I explored the situation, it was clear that she felt very underpaid—and therefore undervalued. Despite this, she enjoyed her work and felt there was a real opportunity for success, and the contradictory situation was clearly stressful for her.

Action: Recognize the different drivers and ensure that both the hygiene and motivation factors are addressed. If you are personally feeling undervalued, establish which of the factors are causing you the most concern and address them one at a time.

Further commentary: The 2x2 matrix also polarizes the suggestion that the two scales are independent, and it isn't that simple, of course. Beware the top left quadrant, as it is a risky place for an organization to be. This situation can easily arise when economic times are tough and there isn't much free cash around. Promotions without rewards can become more common, and while this may be fine in the short term, over a longer period the possibility that this may lead to dissatisfaction is a factor the organization must consider.

Dissatisfaction

	High *(Bad)*	**Low** *(Good)*
High *(Good)*	**Danger** An employee who is dissatisfied with pay or other basic elements, but who is highly motivated and may have received recognition or more responsibility. This quadrant can get full during hard times as employees get promoted but not paid to match the promotion. **Action** Be aware of the possibilities this quadrant represents and establish recovery actions as things improve. The organization could easily lose these employees.	**Ideal** An employee who is OK with pay or other basic elements, is highly motivated and may have received recognition or more responsibility. **Action** Maintain.
Low *(Bad)*	**Rebellion** An employee who is dissatisfied with pay or other basic elements and has not received recognition or other motivators. If the employee can get another job, she is likely to leave. If not, she will demoralize her colleagues. **Action** Sort out the hygiene factors first.	**Waste** An employee who is OK with pay or other basic elements but has not received recognition or other motivators. If the employee is a high flyer, she may leave as she will feel that there is no opportunity for her in the organization. In any case, the organization is missing the opportunity to get the best from this person. **Action** Educate the employee's manager on the importance of Herzberg's motivators and the ease with which they can be applied.

Satisfaction or Motivation (row labels High/Good, Low/Bad on left)

Leadership versus management

Context: Management indicates the competencies associated with maintaining performance and stable operations. These competencies include project management skills (planning for ongoing operations, etc.), understanding measures and controls and being able to apply them, reporting business performance accurately, drawing conclusions, and acting on those conclusions in an appropriate manner.

Leadership is the manifestation of skills associated with making change. A leader can see and articulate a future not yet apparent to others (visionary), and has the ability to communicate not just the vision, but also the required enthusiasm and energy to move towards a changed reality.

The difference between management and leadership is often hidden. Many companies use the term "leader" or "leadership" to mean any level of supervision, whether tactical or visionary, and it has led to the undervaluing of management skills. The consequence of this undervaluing has been less focus on basic management and supervisory skill training; this development became clear to me when I was mentoring an individual with outstanding leadership skills but an immature ability to make it a reality—he was in the bottom right quadrant of the 2x2 matrix.

Key Drivers:
1. Level of leadership skills
2. Level of management skills

Consequence: None of the quadrants of this matrix is necessarily a bad place to be, unless you don't want to be there. However, the bottom right is a place that could readily cause a loss of confidence in new leaders, which would result in a lost opportunity, and can be easily avoided.

Action: Train and prepare your leaders and managers prior to promotion, and then mentor and coach them after the promotion.

Further commentary: There is a glamour associated with leadership that has caused management skills to be underrated and underdeveloped. It is in fashion to use the term "leader" to mean almost anything from first-line supervisor to CEO. And all of those may be true. However, the same honor should apply to the term "manager."

Leadership Skills

	Low	High
High	**Business as usual** An individual with a good control of deliverables (e.g., contract requirements): a good "business as usual" manager. He will need strong controls in place to maintain deliverables and may find it hard to get the extra mile from people. He may tend to supervise closely, which can limit employee growth. **Action** Ensure that individuals with an aspiration to improve their leadership skills have the opportunity to do so. Training, coaching and mentoring, and job change are all possibilities.	**Balanced** A person with good control of both detailed and broader deliverables and who will have the ability to anticipate requirements and to lead into the unknown. He will often have the confidence to allow his employees to take risks. **Action** Maintain
Low	**Worker** This is a worker bee. The lifeblood of every business. If he is promoted without training, and therefore with weak management skills, the employee can find himself in the Crisis quadrant. Once there, the path to improve either management or leadership skills can become obscured. **Action** Ensure that individuals about to be promoted are trained beforehand wherever possible. Encourage him to seek a mentor or coach.	**Crisis** An individual with good visibility of where the organization needs to get to and the enthusiasm to lead. His weak management skills will cause a limited control over current deliverables and can lead to crises. This can be a very demotivating situation, with limited opportunities to celebrate success. **Action** Assign a mentor or coach. Training would be a good next step. His current supervisor may also need support to help them recognize such crises before they occur.

Management Skills (row axis label)

Leader power, organizational trust, and team performance

Context: This 2x2 matrix was created at the same time as the *"Boss says"* versus *personal accountability* matrix. It involves the same scenario and the same people. You will recall that the team leader was referring constantly to her boss, drawing on the boss' power rather than using her own. By doing so, she reduced her own power and credibility yet further. Added to that, the team involved had very low trust between members of the team, and to other interfacing teams.

Key Drivers:

1. The trust evident in the team

2. The power of the leader

Consequence: A highly trusting team and an ineffective leader can be a dangerous combination because the team will develop such strong empathy with each other that the team processes dominate the task. Initial appearances will be good, and performance will be fine, provided the team cohesion is not threatened.

The most assertive action is needed when a team or organization finds itself in the bottom left quadrant. The leader should be replaced if the situation is to be recovered.

Action: Replace the leader quickly if you believe the position is unsalvageable. A temporary situation will not help.

Build trust among the team members. There is a lot of management material on building trust available. There are also organization-developing or team-building methods that can help.

A key action is to ensure that personal objectives and team objectives are aligned. Make sure you know what the individuals in your team aspire to, what motivates them, and what demands they have to manage outside of work. Aligning individuals' personal goals and the team or organizational goals is an effort that will repay you.

Further commentary: Having power does not mean you have to wield it, but lacking it makes the job much more difficult. A highly trusting team with a powerful leader is a very effective combination.

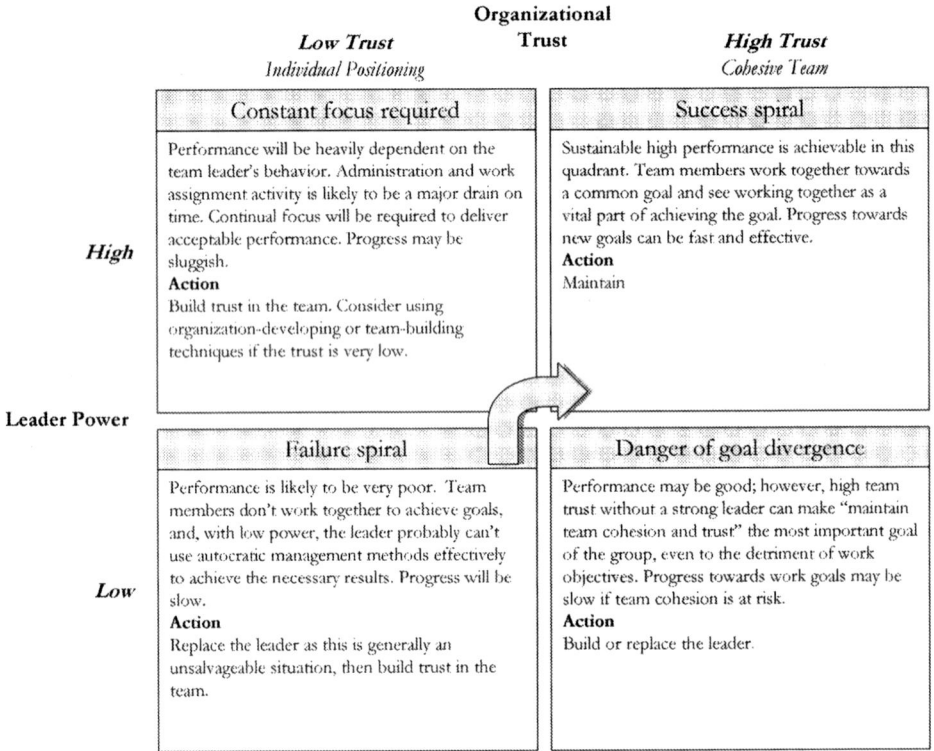

Organizational Trust

	Low Trust *Individual Positioning*	*High Trust* *Cohesive Team*
High	**Constant focus required** Performance will be heavily dependent on the team leader's behavior. Administration and work assignment activity is likely to be a major drain on time. Continual focus will be required to deliver acceptable performance. Progress may be sluggish. **Action** Build trust in the team. Consider using organization-developing or team-building techniques if the trust is very low.	**Success spiral** Sustainable high performance is achievable in this quadrant. Team members work together towards a common goal and see working together as a vital part of achieving the goal. Progress towards new goals can be fast and effective. **Action** Maintain
Low	**Failure spiral** Performance is likely to be very poor. Team members don't work together to achieve goals, and, with low power, the leader probably can't use autocratic management methods effectively to achieve the necessary results. Progress will be slow. **Action** Replace the leader as this is generally an unsalvageable situation, then build trust in the team.	**Danger of goal divergence** Performance may be good; however, high team trust without a strong leader can make "maintain team cohesion and trust" the most important goal of the group, even to the detriment of work objectives. Progress towards work goals may be slow if team cohesion is at risk. **Action** Build or replace the leader.

Leader Power

Who, how, and what

Context: The following matrix was created during an exercise to pull together many disparate groups who were ostensibly working together but, in practice, were working unilaterally.

While any conversation was active about the importance of working together and developing a coordinated shared plan, everyone agreed. However, as soon as they left the room, the agreement disappeared as if the conversation had never happened. Any attempted change in process, for example, was like elastic: it just snapped back to the previous situation.

It transpired that much of the behavior was due to a combination of self-preservation attitudes and no previous experience of consistent processes or standards.

Three elements were interwoven:

1. *Who* performs the task—this was a complex area due to a series of reorganizations that had occurred over the previous months, and a shared sense of belonging was weak.

2. *What* they did—the outcome they were expected to deliver.

3. *How* they did the task—the methods and processes that they used. This was also impacted by the reorganizations, which included an acquisition, and the variations in working practices that that brings.

Key Drivers: To force the polarization of the three elements mentioned above, this combination was explored:

1. *Who* embedded with *What*: an individual has a strong connection to the outcome and is accountable for the results.

2. *What* embedded with *How*: the result is the outcome of an agreed process.

Consequence: In the top right quadrant of the matrix that follows, the deliverable (WHAT) and the method (HOW) are fixed, and the person (WHO) who executes the method is variable. Clearly, this is a sustainable place to be, and the results should be consistent even if the people change. You can see that the other quadrants are all less desirable than the one at the top right.

In the situation that spawned this matrix, many functions fell into the bottom left quadrant.

Action: Breaking the undesirable links between *What* and *Who* almost always means moving people, whether moving them into other roles within the same organization or out of the scenario altogether. Reward the behavior you want to have by acknowledging compliance to the *How* wherever it occurs.

Further commentary: If you are in the bottom left quadrant and want to be in the top right, which way should you go round? I propose that you go around the bottom. While the bottom right quadrant is a very dangerous place to be, with strong change management in place, you can keep the process moving and avoid getting stuck there. Moving into the top left quadrant may be like climbing into a pot of glue—the situation is rigid and difficult to change. Maintaining progress to the top right will be difficult.

**_Who_ Embedded
with the _What_**

	Yes	No
	Rigidity	**Sustainability**
Yes	*How*, *What*, and *Who* are all locked together because the employees have strong ownership of the deliverables they are responsible for and are performing the task in a very specific, personal way. Change is difficult because the strong ownership will tend to prevent compromise or experiments. If change starts, progress may be slow as activities revert to the preferred methods. **Action** This situation is so rigid that a complete change of players may be necessary in order to move into the Sustainability quadrant.	*What* and *How* are tied together, as the deliverables and the processes to create them are standard. *Who* can change. This situation is stable, and the quality of the deliverable is generally independent of the individual performing the task, provided they meet the required skill level. With effective operational controls in place, good progress can be made. **Action** Maintain.
What Embedded with the _How_		
	Do it my way	**Chaos**
No	*What* and *Who* are tied together as the individual has strong ownership for the deliverables. *How* can change as there is no formal process for this function. Individuals are in charge of their deliverables and achieve results in any way they choose. Unilateral progress may be fast and in the right direction, but it is not necessarily sustainable and can be very weak if an individual leaves the position. **Action** Break the *What* and the *Who* apart, perhaps by swapping people's roles about.	*How*, *What*, and *Who* can all move about. There will be fast random changes as there is a quick reaction to almost any stimulus. No progress will be made, but a lot of noise will be generated which may be mistaken for progress. **Action** Lock the *What* and the *How*, by building a strong reward system around compliance to process, for example.

True but not relevant?

Context: I'm sure you will remember times when you have been listening to someone talking at length about something, and you eventually ask, "Why are you telling me this?" Often enough, the reply is, "But it's true!"

Key Drivers:

1. Truth of a statement
2. Relevance of a statement

Consequence: Discussing true but irrelevant subjects happens by accident a great deal.

Action: Challenge the relevance of the topic and steer the conversation back to an area that needs attention.

Further commentary: While challenging relevance is a good step, be prepared to allow useful discussion even when it is not aligned with your agenda. It is good to permit exploring of a valuable area, just be sure that you have made a decision to do so rather than slipping into it accidentally and achieving nothing useful in your meeting.

Introducing a "true but irrelevant" comment is effective if you want to disrupt a discussion—watch out for its deliberate use. You may notice that someone will introduce something that is both important and true, but irrelevant to the current context. This can easily steer the conversation away from the topic you are trying to discuss.

An exercise for you to try: In a meeting dealing with a time-sensitive topic (staffing or scheduling perhaps), say in a loud and concerned voice, "but it's August!" (use the current month). This is patently true. Your loud and concerned voice has made it important and therefore relevant. It is highly likely the meeting will suddenly start talking about August, or the date in some form. When you see how easy this tactic is to use, you may more readily notice someone else using this tactic to derail a meeting.

True

	No	**Yes**

	Threat	**Terrific**
Yes	If the lack of truth is not visible, the relevance may cause exploration of a topic which is not leading anywhere useful. **Action** Validate the truth of data on which you will rely.	Valuable discussion will occur. **Action** Continue to explore the topic.

Relevant

	Trash	**Time wasting**
No	To spend time discussing something that is neither true nor relevant is a waste of time. **Action** End the discussion.	The truth of the topic can be used as justification for the discussion, which wastes time. **Action** Challenge the relevance of the topic, and do not permit "But it's true!" as the sole reason for continuing the conversation. This is the quadrant that makes some processes so heavy. If a subject isn't relevant, cut it out.

CHAPTER 4

SITUATIONAL

You get what you inspect, not what you expect

Context: A few years ago, I heard our chief executive say, "You get what you inspect, not what you expect." I thought about the phrase and decided that you need to consider both aspects: expectations and inspections.

Key Drivers:
1. Clarity of target or expectation
2. Strength of the inspection process

Consequence: Strong inspection of a vague target can be very expensive and a waste of money. It may feel fine; nicely done reports, especially with convincing graphs, can hide a multitude of irrelevancies and inappropriate actions.

Action: Ensure that you have a clear target, with both process-based and output-based metrics, and that you are doing what you planned to do. Make sure that the actions you are taking (reflected in the process-based metrics) are having the result that you intended.

If you think you may be in the bottom left corner of the matrix, improve the target before improving the inspection. You really don't want to end up in the top left quadrant.

Further commentary: Putting strong inspection in place when the target is unclear can be expensive—and is easy to do by accident. The same target can be very clear to one person and ambiguous to another due to their role or experience. A common understanding of a target is essential if multiple parts of an organization contribute to the outcome.

Target or Expectation

	Vague	*Clear*
Strong	**Rework, rework, rework** The target may be visible but is not specific and depends on interpretation. Conclusions may change each time performance is compared to target. Corrective action will be prompt, but may be different after each inspection and contradict previous actions. Rework is likely to be extensive based on varying interpretations. Confidence that the target will be met varies. In any case, what's the target? **Action** Make the target clear, using both process- and output-based metrics. Adjust the inspection.	**Good progress** The target is visible and clear, and inspection is strong. Corrective action will be prompt and specific, and rework will be minimal because each inspection will be based on the same interpretation of the target. Confidence will be high that the performance assessment is accurate and, with appropriate corrective actions plans, that the target will be met. **Action** Maintain.
Inspection		
Weak	**No progress** The target may be visible but is not specific and depends on interpretation. As inspection is weak, very little corrective action will be taken. Rework is likely to be driven by failures rather than measures of quality. Confidence that the target will be met is very low. In any case, what's the target? **Action** First make the target clear, using both process- and output-based metrics.	**Slow progress** The target is visible and clear, however it is not inspected, and corrective actions will be delayed. The clarity of the target means that actions will tend to be specific when they are undertaken. Corrective actions will often be driven by failures rather than the results of inspections. Confidence that the target will be met will run from medium to low and will be strongly affected by the pace of activities. **Action** Improve the inspection.

New thinking versus recycled thinking

Context: I have seen great new ideas fall by the wayside and, conversely, rehashed old ideas gather accolades and applause. Why is this happening? How can we be so enthusiastic about the presentation of an old idea and give so little attention to a new one?

Partly this happens because there is comfort in familiarity, but there is also another factor at play: the presentation of the materials.

Key Drivers:

1. The idea, or the content of a concept
2. The presentation of the idea

Consequence: We miss opportunities when new ideas are presented so poorly then their real value is lost, and we spend money polishing and implementing old methods that—if they were valuable at all—the value has already been gleaned from them.

Action: Ensure that an old idea in a shiny package isn't spending your money. Change is always expensive, regardless of the outcome of the change. If you have a great idea, seek help to be sure that it is presented in the best way possible. Don't rely on an idea's intrinsic value to sell it.

Further commentary: You could reasonably point out that much of this book falls into the top left quadrant of the matrix: it is a recycling of what we already know in a form that is easily consumed. You would be right.

One reason to become good at the presentation is so that when you develop a new concept, you are more likely to be able to work in the top right quadrant than in the bottom right.

**Status of the
Concept**

	Rework of an Existing Concept	*New Concept*
Focused, Sharp and Clear	**After-dinner speaker circuit** The materials produced by the rework may be plausible and inspiring and can result in action being. There is likely to be a minimal change if it truly is a rework, as the benefits of this concept may have been gathered before. By attempting a change, the costs of change will be incurred but they are likely to deliver low returns. **Action** Ensure that the change is properly analyzed so that the real change, if any, emerges. Ensure that the value of the action is established. If the value isn't high enough, don't do it.	**Catalyst for change** A new idea may be rejected as impossible, hence the importance of presenting such a concept effectively. If the idea is of real business value and supported by a change program, a substantial benefit may be achievable. Competitive advantage can be achieved by being the first to embrace a new concept. **Action** Ensure that the potential change is properly analyzed and that the value of any proposed action is established. If the value isn't high enough, don't do it.
Muddled, Mixed and Overprocessed	**Porridge** An old concept can often live a long life in the guise of continuous improvement, being continually re-presented and re-drawn. This is an unnecessary expense as nothing really changes other than documentation. **Action** Examine the activities, and if nothing significant is changing, stop the rework and revisit less often.	**Missed opportunity** A new direction or opportunity that looks like porridge won't get the attention that it needs to be properly explored. It becomes a wasted expense. **Action** Review the possibility of moving to the quadrant above to freshen up the context of the change.

Presentation and Thinking

Making a change

Context: The following matrix emerged while I was working with a group of people who were lumbering through a complex process for a relatively simple and low-risk change.

"We always do it this way. It works," they explained when I asked them why they were using the process.

"A missed opportunity for taking a risk and learning," I thought.

Key Drivers:

1. Complexity of the change
2. Method used to manage the change

Consequence: Using a complex methodology for a simple change can make the situation more expensive and riskier than it needs to be. A great deal of energy is expended in the team processes—energy that is *not* being expended on the change itself.

Action: Assess the situation and select a methodology suited to the complexity. Seek mentoring to learn an appropriate method if it is not within your current armory.

Further commentary: You will notice that both quadrants associated with the complex change are marked with "danger." Complex change is never easy.

Type of Change

	Simple	*Complex*
Familiar	**Potential for overkill** Players can move fast because the processes the team uses are familiar to them. If the process is complex and the change is simple, the overkill can make employees feel weary and unnecessarily overloaded. **Action** If you have started and can't change the methodology, you may benefit from asking an experienced colleague to review your change plan and cut out unnecessary steps.	**Play-it-again danger** Players can move fast as the processes the team uses are familiar. There is danger that the change situation will be reviewed with past changes in mind and that assumptions may take the place of conclusions. This may be a lost opportunity of embracing change with change and the innovation that this can spawn. **Action** Ensure that the change process embraces an independent review, and ensure that any assumptions are challenged.
Unfamiliar	**Learning opportunity** This situation provides a good opportunity for people to widen their repertoires of tools and methods in a relatively risk-free way. Unless the change required is very urgent, there are no obvious disadvantages of this quadrant. **Action** Take the opportunity to learn.	**Do-it-twice danger** Change in processes can lead to innovative thinking and can be beneficial. The team making the change are also accepting change, making them more sensitive to the feelings of the recipients of the main change. There is a danger that using new processes will slow down the change team. Strong governance is needed to notice early signs of problems and take action to mitigate the danger. **Action** Seek external review of governance, and catch early slippage or risks.

Method Used to Manage the Change

Quality, speed, process, and project

Context: While investigating operational problems—a failure of a production machine, for example—a repetitive and contradictory situation became apparent. It was getting confusing. Some problems were obviously being caused by close adherence to process when the situation was novel and outside the realm of the current process, and rapid results were needed. Other problems rose out of the combination of a poor process structure and a project approach—addressing all activities as if they were being done for the first time.

Both problems were visible at the same time.

Key Drivers:

1. What is your key challenge? Quality or Speed?

2. Which is best? A process approach or a project approach?

Consequence: Taking the wrong approach can cause you to go too slowly for your needs or cause you to run below the quality level that you need.

Action: I suggest that there isn't one "best" answer. The answer is critically linked to the most important or urgent outcome that you require (speed or quality). Recognize that the pressures change over time and the challenge is not, in fact, "Which?" The challenge is when and how to switch.

Further commentary: The possibility that "diagonal corners"—in this example top right and bottom left—in a 2x2 matrix are both good places to be became obvious during the development of this matrix. It is also relevant that the same organization, at different times, could benefit from different corners.

Primary Driver

	Speed	*Quality*
Process-Driven	**Can be too slow** Benefits of speed will be missed when you have a short window of opportunity. Process-driven situations can be self-perpetuating with constant rewrites and improvements of processes, which can easily become overcomplex and are meaningful only to the authors. **Action** When speed is the primary driver and a process-driven approach is necessary, consider an external project-focused mentor.	**Can be a good match** Sustainability and repeatability are considered. Process-driven situations can be self-perpetuating with constant rewrites and improvements of processes, which can easily become overcomplex and are meaningful only to the authors. **Action** Maintain while this is a good match. Be alert to the need to swap corners.
Project-Driven	**Can be a good match** The quality or quantity of what is delivered may be at risk if the date-driven perspective becomes critical. Project-driven situations can produce fragmented outputs, especially if project managers change. Operations can become unwieldy if much reworking or redesigning is necessary. **Action** Maintain while this is a good match. Be alert to the need to swap corners.	**Can be too short-term focused** Speedy results that do not support repeatability can mean operational inefficiencies or rework as the operational problems materialize. Project-driven situations can produce fragmented outputs, especially if project managers change. Operations can become unwieldy if much reworking or redesigning is necessary. **Action** When quality is the primary driver and a project-driven approach is necessary, consider an external operational-focused mentor.

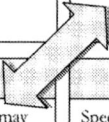

Action Focus (row axis label, positioned left of the table)

Time and space communications

Context: For a long period of time, I worked in different time zones from my colleagues and spent a lot of time attending teleconferences outside of my normal working hours, often late into the evening. It was infuriating that I was spending my leisure time in teleconferences with people who were turning up late, talking trivia, and otherwise behaving normally because it was mid-afternoon for them.

There was an additional challenge associated with such meetings: since some people were on a telephone and others in a room together, the telephone attendees were often relegated to listening to a meeting as opposed to being part of the meeting.

Key Drivers:

1. The place of the communication

2. The time of the communication

Consequence: The potential value of the communication may not be achieved, subsequently impacting the outcome originally sought by the meeting. Additionally, there are cost implications of choosing the wrong type of meeting. For example, a face-to-face meeting for a topic that could be dealt with in e-mail is a waste of money.

Action: Consider and select the most appropriate communication method. If the answer is a teleconference, be cognizant of those attending via the telephone—are they fully engaged in the meeting? Give special consideration to those for whom the meeting takes place outside of normal working hours.

Further commentary: The bottom left quadrant is an interesting one that I have continued to explore by working with colleagues around the world. "But that's bottom, right?" you might ask. Well yes, it is, but virtual work—which makes location irrelevant—opens up the opportunity for passing work between people so that progress on the same task can continue in much the same way that traditional shift workers pass responsibility on to the next shift or a coworker. Perhaps there's another variation here in which location becomes more closely aligned with a role or task.

Location

	Same	*Different*
Same	**Face-to-face meetings** This method is often the most successful for complex communications and is ethically required for certain types of communication. However, face-to-face meetings can be expensive if travel is required. These meetings can be longer than some of the other options because normal social behaviors such as catching-up occur. **Action** Ensure that the maximum value is gleaned from these expensive events and assess the purpose and structure of the meeting accordingly.	**Teleconferences** As travel is avoided, teleconferences are cheaper than face-to-face meetings, and their participants can explain more complex concepts than they can via e-mail. However, the convenience of all attendees to attend is sometimes ignored, and inconsiderate times can be selected. A mixture of a face-to-face meeting and a teleconference can be ineffective, with those on the phone often relegated to an observer role. **Action** Hold the meeting twice, if necessary, to reasonably accommodate all time zones.
Different	**Shift or job-share handovers** A specific type of communication which generally requires a structured role and standard methods. This type of communication enables functions to be performed continually, with the involvement of many different people. However, the consistency required can limit or slow the introduction of improvements. **Action** Consider the opportunity to apply a follow-the-sun concept, in which value is added continually.	**E-mail** E-mail correspondence is independent of time and place, and communications can be planned and improved before being sent, providing an opportunity to clarify and support complex statements. Unfortunately, since comprehension is the recipient's activity alone, different interpretations can easily occur. The ease of sending communications via e-mail can result in the sharing of massive amounts of low-value data. **Action** Recognize that complex communications benefit from an additional method such as a phone call.

Here **Time** spans the rows: *Same* (top row) and *Different* (bottom row).

Progress against plan versus results achieved

Context: When you are managing a project, you can measure two things:

- Are you doing what you said you would do?
- Are those actions producing the results that you need?

We all know that what you do has a relationship to the results you get. Very simplistically put, if you execute a plan, the results of those actions will follow. The problem is that it isn't a simple relationship, and to ensure that you get the results you require, you need to do more than verify that you are doing what you planned to do.

Key Drivers:

1. Progress against plan
2. Progress against target results

Consequence: Measuring progress against plan with no tracking of results (or conversely, measuring results but not the plan) can lead to a completed plan with inadequate results. Ultimately, you deprive yourself of any early-warning signals of shortfall results.

Action: Continually keep your mind on both the results and the appropriateness of the plan. Do not permit the two to diverge. When early-warning signs manifest themselves, take action to assess the situation and to remedy it.

Further commentary: If the results you are looking for can only be properly measured at the end of the plan, you may need to generate a form of interim output, even if the project costs more to produce it, to ensure that you get the required results.

If you are asked to work on a troubled project and you don't know where you are on the matrix, don't waste time working it out. Assume that you are in the bottom right quadrant and assess the adequacy of the plan.

Progress Against Plan

	Running Late	On Schedule
	Danger	**Ideal**
On Target	The plan running behind schedule may affect the results later, even though they look fine now. **Action** Recommit to results and complete a risk analysis. What is the root cause of the delay? Can it be addressed? Identify ways to get back on plan.	This is the best quadrant to be in, where the plan is being executed on time and the expected results are materializing. **Action** Recommit to results and complete a risk analysis. Seek opportunities to accelerate the plan so that the results are delivered ahead of time or delivered with a higher level of quality.
	Mitigate	**Inadequate**
Running Below Target	Assess whether getting back on plan will remedy the shortfall in results. **Action** What is the root cause of the delay? Can it be addressed? Identify ways to get back on plan. Will addressing the delay adequately meet the target shortfall? Assess actions to meet target and replan if necessary. Recommit to results and complete a risk analysis.	The plan is inadequate as demonstrated by being on schedule, but the results are not materializing. **Action** Aggressively reassess actions to meet the target. Replan accordingly. A strategic review is advisable. Seek help from someone who is an expert and has not been involved to date. The expert's independent view will be invaluable. Recommit to results and complete a risk analysis.

Progress Against Target Results (row label spanning left side)

Satisfaction versus dissatisfaction for the client

Context: This is a variation of the earlier Herzberg matrix used in the section titled "Satisfaction versus dissatisfaction for the employee," reworked for clients: I have reframed the Herzberg ideas to say:

Basic employee factors such as pay are the equivalent of the basic contracted services for a client:

- If you do these poorly, you have an unhappy client.

- If you do them well, you have a neutral client. Doing what someone is paying you to do doesn't make the buyer happy; it just stops them from being unhappy.

The basic elements are tangible things and can easily be measured and reported against.

Improving the satisfaction of a client comes from more interesting things, such as innovation, creativity, and flexibility. These are intangible things and are often difficult to target or measure.

Key Drivers:

1. Dissatisfaction
2. Satisfaction

Consequence: To maximize your chances of growing your business, you need to do, at a minimum, what you are currently being paid to do. This will remove a source of dissatisfaction, and provide you with a neutral starting point. Unless it is difficult to change suppliers, this will not provide you with a strong growth platform, and some means of satisfying your client is needed.

Action: If you have any problems with the service—if dissatisfaction is high— you must fix the problems with the service. Once they are addressed, consider options to increase satisfaction, such as exploring ideas to help your client grow his business.

Further commentary: If you have innovative new products under development, recognize that, to have a conversation with your existing clients about those products, it would be best for you to be in the top right quadrant. To get there, you should deliver the required service competently and demonstrate an ability to be innovative.

Dissatisfaction
Driven by Meeting Contacted Services

	High *(Bad)*	**Low** *(Good)*
High *(Good)*	**Bemused** You are delivering poor or unreliable service, but you are also meeting other less tangible expectations. Perhaps you are being innovative and creative and helping the client grow his business. **Action** Fix the service.	**Growth** A desirable place to be. Generally, this indicates both good service and a strong relationship, meeting both tangible and intangible expectations. **Action** Continue and build.
Low *(Bad)*	**Danger** This is a very dangerous quadrant to be in. Termination or non-renewal is a clear possibility. You are meeting neither service expectations nor the more intangible causes of satisfaction. **Action** Fix the service first.	**Static** You probably have good service, but you are not in a growth situation. While this is a viable quadrant to remain in, exploring possible growth opportunities is also an option. **Action** If there is opportunity to grow the business, you should consider actions to raise the client's satisfaction.

Satisfaction
Driven by Innovation, Creativity and Flexibility

Changing the Who or the What or both

Context: If you change neither the person doing a task nor the methods they are using, you should not expect any change to the outcome.

This is so obvious that you must wonder why I have stated it. Still, I see this happening time after time. For example, a man was appointed to a similar role that he had held previously despite his mediocre performance in that role. Where a change is required but neither the people nor the methods are reviewed, everyone just does everything the same, though perhaps they do it faster.

Key Drivers:

1. The behaviors, or the things people do; for example, the processes they use

2. The people who execute the processes

Consequence: Making a change "just in case it helps" sounds like a poor tactic, however this is what is happening if a change is made without an assessment of what change needs to be made.

Action: Establish the cause of the under-performance and address it. Clarifying the problem is important and is part of the solution. Clarification alone will not address issues of competence or weak processes.

Further commentary: This 2x2 matrix has proved especially helpful in encouraging a structured review of situations in which performance is sluggish. The analysis has increased the likelihood that any action will be adequate.

What
The Behaviors

	Same	Different
Different	**Addresses incompetence** This will fix the problem if the original challenge was incompetence and if the new person is competent in the behaviors. There is a danger in that the change, as with most changes, will introduce noise into the system and disguise a continuation of the problem. **Action** Keep a close watch on the situation and act if it is not improving.	**Addresses a crisis** This will fix the problem if the behaviors were inappropriate and the desired actions are beyond the capability of the employee. To ensure success, a review should take place to identify the problem and outline a solution **Action** Measure progress and act promptly if corrective action is needed.
Same	**Addresses nothing** This will fix nothing. However keeping things the same is an option that is frequently selected either as another chance for the current employee to sort things out, or because the solution is not yet clear. **Action** If you need to change things, an initial step could be to assign a mentor to help the employee explore the problem and propose a solution.	**Addresses poor process** This will work when the process was wrong and has been corrected. It will work best if the employee identified the process error in the first place and sought to correct it. If he was following an inadequate process without challenging it, it may be best to move to the "Addresses a crisis" quadrant. **Action** If you stay in this quadrant, monitor the situation closely and act promptly if it does not improve.

Who (label appears at left between the two rows)

Collaborative implementation

Context: While discussing change management with a colleague, they commented on the power I wield to ensure that a decision is implemented. They were concerned that they could not exert such power themselves as they worked in a very collaborative organization. I challenged them on this point and made the assertion, "You can make decisions collaboratively, but you can't implement them collaboratively—that is like not making a decision."

Subsequently, I decided to explore this a bit further. Was this assertion too glib, too naïve? Did the possibility of collaborative implementation exist as a realistic and effective option?

By observing a number of different change programs—effective and otherwise—the assertion I made was shown to be sound.

Key Drivers:
1. The decision-making process
2. The decision-implementing process

Consequence: The slowest situations will be those in which a decision is made collaboratively and then implemented collaboratively. The level of urgency this combination carries is very low.

A great deal depends on your viewpoint. If you agree with the change, especially if you are enthusiastic about it, it may not matter which implementation method is used. Where a change is unpalatable, collaborative implementation would not be successful.

Action: Carefully consider the most effective way to make and implement a decision. Time spent during the decision-making process to make the decision more attractive may enable a faster implementation.

Further commentary: As mentioned in the matrix, there are certain circumstances in which collaborative implementation can be useful in making an autocratically made decision more acceptable.

Making Decisions

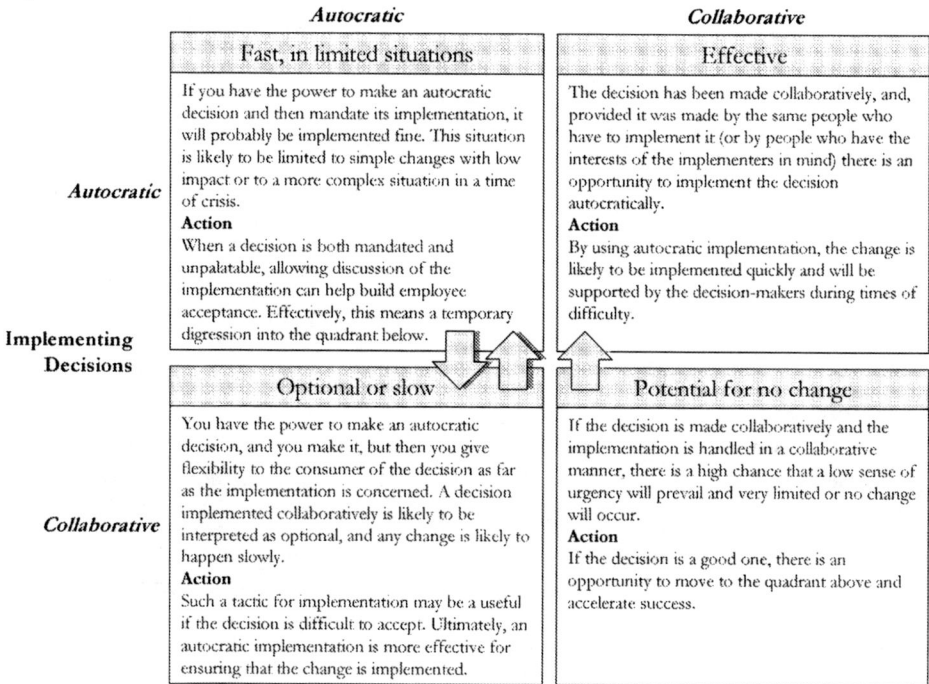

Implementing Decisions	*Autocratic*	*Collaborative*
Autocratic	**Fast, in limited situations** If you have the power to make an autocratic decision and then mandate its implementation, it will probably be implemented fine. This situation is likely to be limited to simple changes with low impact or to a more complex situation in a time of crisis. **Action** When a decision is both mandated and unpalatable, allowing discussion of the implementation can help build employee acceptance. Effectively, this means a temporary digression into the quadrant below.	**Effective** The decision has been made collaboratively, and, provided it was made by the same people who have to implement it (or by people who have the interests of the implementers in mind) there is an opportunity to implement the decision autocratically. **Action** By using autocratic implementation, the change is likely to be implemented quickly and will be supported by the decision-makers during times of difficulty.
Collaborative	**Optional or slow** You have the power to make an autocratic decision, and you make it, but then you give flexibility to the consumer of the decision as far as the implementation is concerned. A decision implemented collaboratively is likely to be interpreted as optional, and any change is likely to happen slowly. **Action** Such a tactic for implementation may be a useful if the decision is difficult to accept. Ultimately, an autocratic implementation is more effective for ensuring that the change is implemented.	**Potential for no change** If the decision is made collaboratively and the implementation is handled in a collaborative manner, there is a high chance that a low sense of urgency will prevail and very limited or no change will occur. **Action** If the decision is a good one, there is an opportunity to move to the quadrant above and accelerate success.

CHAPTER 5

MOVING FORWARD

This book has brought together a number of 2x2 matrix explorations, all representing real situations. In some cases, the 2x2 matrix study helped resolve a particular circumstance. In others, the analysis was done after the event and was used as an educational tool. Perhaps it was used in a similar situation that occurred later.

The most important point, though, is that none of these answers is right. Each only reflects my viewpoint at that particular time. These answers are not offered here as the correct answers; they are offered as examples of how exploring a situation that is causing concern can be a valuable thing to do.

Observing and analyzing, especially in less stressful times, will improve your skills, and you will find yourself more able to use those skills in times of crisis. You will find it very helpful, both personally and professionally, to be able to use those skills when many others are less able to cope.

The methods I have described will help you to:

- Assimilate information quickly and clearly
- Identify the key drivers of the situation
- Propose consequences caused by any two of those drivers
- Recommend actions that could help to address the symptoms or the cause.

Practice definitely helps, so don't get downhearted if the first few 2x2 matrices you produce are vague or of limited value. Keep going and make sure you record all your attempts. You will find yourself returning to them, and that will indicate when you have made an original and useful start.

As you establish the 2x2 matrices that are of value to you, I suggest that you include them in the next section to create a record of your successes and a useful handbook for the future.

Context:

Key Drivers:

  1.

  2.

Consequence:

Action:

Further commentary:

Context:

Key Drivers:

    1.

    2.

Consequence:

Action:

Further commentary:

Context:

Key Drivers:

    1.

    2.

Consequence:

Action:

Further commentary:

Context:

Key Drivers:

    1.

    2.

Consequence:

Action:

Further commentary:

Context:

Key Drivers:

　　1.

　　2.

Consequence:

Action:

Further commentary:

Context:

Key Drivers:

1.

2.

Consequence:

Action:

Further commentary:

Context:

Key Drivers:

    1.

    2.

Consequence:

Action:

Further commentary:

Context:

Key Drivers:

    1.

    2.

Consequence:

Action:

Further commentary:

Context:

Key Drivers:

    1.

    2.

Consequence:

Action:

Further commentary:

Context:

Key Drivers:

    1.

    2.

Consequence:

Action:

Further commentary:

Context:

Key Drivers:

    1.

    2.

Consequence:

Action:

Further commentary:

BIBLIOGRAPHY

Herzberg, F., B. Maunser, and B. Synderman. *The Motivation to Work.* New York: Wiley, 1959.

Vroom, V. H., and P. W. Yetton. *Leadership and Decision-Making.* Pittsburgh: University of Pittsburgh Press, 1973.

978-0-595-42420-7
0-595-42420-1

Printed in the United States
94671LV00004B/508-555/A

9 780595 424207